ROAD BUILDERS

BY B. G. HENNESSY · PICTURES BY SIMMS TABACK

Viking

The artwork was done using
pen and ink, airbrush, and
cut Cello-Tak color sheets.

VIKING
Published by Penguin Group
Penguin Young Readers Group, 345 Hudson Street, New York, New York 10014, U.S.A.
Penguin Books Ltd, 80 Strand, London WC2R ORL, England
Penguin Books Australia Ltd, 250 Camberwell Road, Camberwell, Victoria 3124, Australia
Penguin Books Canada Ltd, 10 Alcorn Avenue, Toronto, Ontario, Canada M4V 3B2
Penguin Books (N.Z.) Ltd, 182-190 Wairau Road, Auckland 10, New Zealand

First published in 1994 by Viking, a division of Penguin Books USA Inc.

10 9 8 7 6 5 4 3 2 1

Special Markets ISBN 9781984837097 Not for Resale

Text copyright © B. G. Hennessy, 1994
Illustrations copyright © Simms Taback, 1994
All rights reserved
Special thanks to Bud Hennessy for his technical advice.

LIBRARY OF CONGRESS CATALOGING-IN-PUBLICATION DATA
Hennessy, B. G. (Barbara G.)
     Road builders / B.G. Hennessy ; illustrated by Simms Taback.   p.   cm.
     ISBN 0-670-83390-8
     1. Road machinery—Juvenile literature.   2. Roads—Design and
construction—Juvenile literature.   [1. Roads—Design and
construction.   2. Road machinery.]   I. Taback, Simms, ill.
II. Title.
TE223.H43   1994   625.7—dc20   93-42248

Manufactured in China
Set in 20 point Futura Medium Condensed

This Imagination Library edition is published by Penguin Young Readers, a division
of Penguin Random House, exclusively for Dolly Parton's Imagination Library,
a not-for-profit program designed to inspire a love of reading and learning, sponsored
in part by The Dollywood Foundation. Penguin's trade editions of this work are
available wherever books are sold.

To my favorite road builders:
Matt, Mark, and Brett
—B. G. H.

To Sean and to Jay Baugher
—S. T.

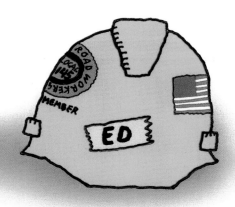

It takes many kinds of trucks to build a road.

Pickup trucks, cement mixers, bulldozers,
dump trucks, backhoes, graders, crane trucks,

power shovels, front loaders, pavers, power rollers, striper trucks, and cherry-picker trucks.

Here are Buddy, John, Ed, Fran, Joe, Jessie, and Chuck.
They are going to build a road.

Buddy is the boss. He follows a plan
that shows where the road is going to be
and tells everyone what to do.

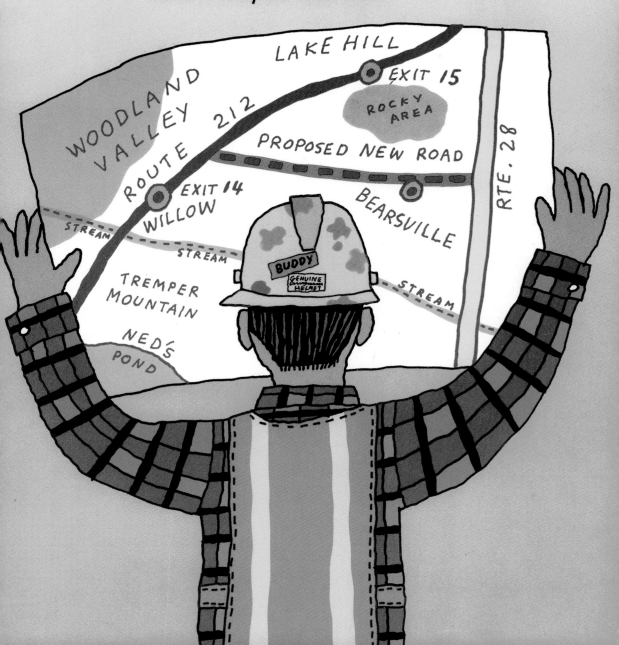

The power shovel scoops and lifts the dirt.

A bulldozer pushes the dirt away.

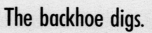

The backhoe digs.

The front loader pushes and carries dirt and rocks,

which the dump trucks carry away.

The grader smooths the ground.

Dump trucks bring in gravel for the roadbed.
A cement mixer pours cement down a chute
to make the gutters at the sides of the road.

Then dump trucks dump asphalt into
the paver truck. Asphalt is a mixture
of stones, stone dust, and gooey tar.
The paver lays the asphalt on the roadbed.

The power roller packs it down
so that the road is smooth.

A truck called a striper paints the lines on the center of the road.

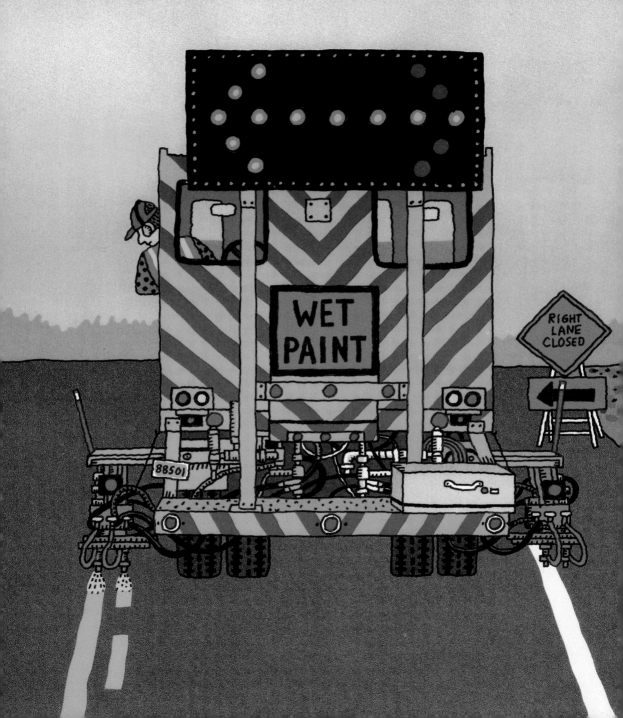

WET PAINT

RIGHT LANE CLOSED

88501

The crane truck raises a sign.

The cherry-picker truck lifts a worker, who puts up the lights.

At last the road is finished.
The road builders are gone.
Now the road is ready.

And here come moving vans, taxicabs,
delivery trucks, motorcycles, school buses, RVs . . .

. . . family cars, fire engines, horse trailers,

soda-bottle trucks, police cars, jeeps, sports cars . . .

... and flatbed trucks carrying the road builders to their next job.